OCULUS

Also by Sally Wen Mao

Mad Honey Symposium

OCULUS

POEMS

Sally Wen Mao

Graywolf Press

This publication is made possible, in part, by the voters of Minnesota through a Minnesota State Arts Board Operating Support grant, thanks to a legislative appropriation from the arts and cultural heritage fund, and a grant from the Wells Fargo Foundation. Significant support has also been provided by Target, the McKnight Foundation, the Lannan Foundation, the Amazon Literary Partnership, and other generous contributions from foundations, corporations, and individuals. To these organizations and individuals we offer our heartfelt thanks.

This book is made possible through a partnership with the College of Saint Benedict, and honors the legacy of S. Mariella Gable, a distinguished teacher at the College. Support has been provided by the Manitou Fund as part of the Warner Reading Program.

Special funding for this title was provided by the Jerome Foundation.

Published by Graywolf Press
212 Third Avenue North, Suite 485
Minneapolis, Minnesota 55401

www.graywolfpress.org

Published in the United States of America

ISBN 978-1-55597-825-9

4 6 8 10 11 9 7 5 3

Library of Congress Control Number: 2018947076

Cover design: Jeenee Lee Design

Cover art: Sally Wen Mao

for all my sisters

Contents

/   //   ///

/   //   ///

"An eye on film, affixed to an unconscious body. The eye sees nothing for the camera has already robbed it of vision . . . It isn't possible to reconstruct a story from this landscape of ruins."

—Yoko Tawada, *The Naked Eye*

"It is on the stage of contaminated desires that we are most pressed to reconsider the politics of recognition."

—Anne Anlin Cheng, *Second Skin*

OCULUS

///   //   /

Ghost Story

Forgive me if the wind stole
the howl from my mouth and whipped
it against your windowpanes.
When I lived, I wanted to be seen.
I built this mansion made of windows
for my prince and me. He feinted,
I knocked—we were apparitions of splendor.
Our dining hall was the Santa Maria Novella.
Our bedroom was the Izumo Shrine.
Our study, a study in tension. Books slid
off the buttresses. We bluffed a life together
on this mattress. When I kissed him,
I kissed a marble statue. It was Apollo,
it was Krishna, it was Ra. Monitor lizards
wandered through the empty halls.
The pianola a stronghold for tarantulas.
We relied on our plasma television
to pull us back to the world again.
Downstairs, the curtains parted, exposing
us to the wolves above. We beamed
our searchlights onto them. Soon
a Technicolor wilderness surrounded
us. Turquoise stags watched us shave
with electric razors. We built new barricades
between ourselves. Our bathroom,
a wallpaper of scars. After he fled
the premises, I unearthed my binoculars
before the mansion was razed. That was the last
time I trusted a body that touched me.
All a ghost wants is to be chained
to a place, to someone who can't forget

her. Every day I try to fight my own
brokenness. But once you are forgotten,
it's not so bad: a heart broken
joins another chorus. Can you hear
the chorus speak? Can you bear
it? The words of apparitions do not belong
to a language. They flit over pines, meaningless,
and shed their skins in your hands.

Oculus

Before I wake, I peruse the dead girl's live
        photo feed. Days ago, she uploaded

her confessions: *I can't bear the sorrow*
        captions her black eyes, gaps across a face

luminescent as snow. I can't bear the snow—
        how it falls, swells over the bridges,

under my clothes, yet I can't be held
        or beheld here, in this barren warren,

this din of ruined objects, peepholes into boring
        scandals. Stockings roll high past hems

as I watch the videos of her boyfriend, cooing:
        behave, darling, so I can make you my wife.

How the dead girl fell, awaiting a hand to hold,
        eyes to behold her as the lights clicked on

and she posed for her picture, long eyelashes
        all wet, legs tapered, bright as thorns.

Her windows overlook Shanghai, curtains drawn
        to cast a shadow over the Huangpu River,

frozen this year into a dry, bloodless
        stalk. Why does the light in the night

promise so much? She wiped her lens
        before she died. The smudge still lives.

I saw it singe the edge of her bed.
        Soon it swallowed the whole burning city.

Occidentalism

A man celebrates erstwhile conquests,
his book locked in a silo, still in print.

I scribble, make Sharpie lines, deface
its text like it defaces me. Outside, grain

fields whisper. Marble lions are silent
yet silver-tongued, with excellent teeth.

In this life I have worshipped so many lies.
Then I workshop them, make them better.

An East India Company, an opium trade,
a war, a treaty, a concession, an occupation,

a man parting the veil covering a woman's
face, his nails prying her lips open. I love

the fragility of a porcelain bowl. How easy
it is, to shatter chinoiserie, like the Han

dynasty urn Ai Weiwei dropped in 1995.
If only recovering the silenced history

is as simple as smashing its container: book,
bowl, celadon spoon. Such objects cross

borders the way our bodies never could.
Instead, we're left with history, its blonde

dust. That bowl is unbreakable. All its ghosts
still shudder through us like small breaths.

The tome of hegemony lives on, circulates
in our libraries, in our bloodstreams. One day,

a girl like me may come across it on a shelf,
pick it up, read about all the ways her body

is a thing. And I won't be there to protect
her, to cross the text out and say: *go ahead*—

rewrite this.

Teledildonics

              haptic
        touches flare   little moths
              or schisms

faraway clavicles   ribs
        a pornography live
                through open
        electrodes
touch your internet through your clothes

        kinesthetic sand
                for kinesthetic toes
kinesthetically fucked
        next to the lifeless reefs
                palm trees
        chafe the skin

maybe I'll spend the rest
        of my life
        with my remote control
under the never-ending sun
                the never-fallow
        the never-breaking

        paradisiacal goggles
my VR headset
        newest stereoscope
                for our millennium

we'll live and love forever
  by the sea that will never drown us
    in the wellness shore
  and the undulating rice fields
where all touch gives pleasure
  all touch is welcome

and nothing will hurt
  and nothing will bruise

Mutant Odalisque

This is not an ode. February's ice razor scalps
    the gingko trees, their hair pulled skyward
        like the ombre roots

of young women. March harrows
    us mottled girls. Vernal equinox:
        a hare harries the chicks, hurries

behind wet haystacks. Livestock.
    Gnats. The glue-traps are gone.

March, ladies. March for your dignity.
    March for your happiness. March, a muss

of lidless eyes. In the forest, a handsome man pisses,
    puissant, luminary's ink leaking on trees.

Penury I furl into the craven lens, in its mirror, a pulse:
    webcam where I kiss my witnesses.

They watch and watch and watch the butcher
    cut, the surgeon mend, they watch the glade
        of crushed femora, they watch my dorsal fin,

they watch my scales dart across the cutting
    board. They watch the way I open, flinch, bent

against the wind that beheads the nimbuses.
    Or April's turning toward ecstatic sob—departure.

Networks freeze, all sloe, all ice. Transmitters
        falter. The cicatrix soaped, cilia and pus
rubbed raw. No machine. I dare
        my witnesses to stick their pencils on me.

Do they marvel at a conquest—
        blue flesh and gills. Do they think of me as soiled
or new soil. Do they take notes in their medical
        journals. Am I their inspiration—O Vesalius, god

of anatomy, is that why they ask so softly for my name.

Live Feed

After I am dead, I will hunt you
      day and night. Pixelated ghosts

will haunt your ears. Trees will crack
      under my digital weight.
            In a minute my arrest

will go live, handcuff you to your bed.
      It's starting: I watch you watch me.
            I watch you lurk me, my starling,

it rolls: I'm the beggar. I shake the train—
      gyrate, move, bare my shoulders, they come
            for me, jostle and flay.

I am a fish and a pariah
      drying in my oubliette.

Release me—share me, my shards
      and my innards—
            reduce me to a watering hole

for your thirst. Thrash
      against my pincers. Undo

yourself, let the oculus
      burn through my clothes, record

every mistake I make.
      I feed you my limbs

in this glass container. I limn
you with this fodder
and you taste.

No Resolution

In December 2012, a father from Queens, Ki Suk Han,
was pushed into the train tracks of an oncoming Q train.
This poem is for his daughter, Ashley Han.

The cover of the magazine. I throw it open.
　　　I throw it out. THIS MAN, announces
the headline. THIS MAN IS ABOUT TO—

Blood broadcasts the story. Noise rakes
　　　the story and pummels it to the ground
until there's nothing left. No story. No man.

No wife and daughter, no life in Queens.
　　　His daughter doesn't speak. She closes
her eyes, and her lids sear the whites beneath.

At the press conference, she hides her hands
　　　inside her hoodie. All the cameras. They point,
they shoot—she reels, she shatters.

A year later I will meet her. We will walk down West 4th,
　　　MacDougal, under the arches on a crisp
October day. We will eat crepes in the East Village,
　　　watch a man play piano in the square.

She will talk about her father—the story
　　　of all our lives—how she didn't have the chance
to connect with him fully, and then suddenly—
　　　it was the story of none of our lives—

and she was 21, an only child, with her father's
          fate on a magazine cover, piled in grocery
stores across America, in low-res, high-res,
          the pixels blurred like smudges on skin.

For now, it is December. The shadows on the platforms
          elongate. I have not yet met her. I turn off the television,
afraid of its heft, its volume, its relationship to gravity.

Lately, I can't go underground without shielding
          my body with my hands. The train whines
and goes. The stories about our lives do not have faces.

Provenance: A Vivisection

"[The Bodies exhibition] is a redemocratization. The human body
is the last remaining nature in a man-made environment."

—*Gunther von Hagens*

I.

You, you are a factory
of muscle. You, you are an empire
of polymer. I recognize myself

in your face, your posture, your severed
epiglottis. Take it off. Take it all off
for us to see: first the clothes,

then the epidermis, then your mouth,
your country, your context. *Provenance*:
a chronology of ownership—

all tautology, for none of our emissaries
have uncovered the tampered body's
histories. The prophet calculates

the profits. Exhibit A: Hottentot Venus,
1810. Pregnant woman from village X,
reclining nude in lit interior. Excision—

watch the womb peeled back,
see what milkless plastic the baby
suckles, how he crows against the vernix

of his mother's plastic gluetrap. Baby,
do you dream of trapezes? Baby, do
you choke on the inchoate cloud?

II.

Gunther von Hagens was born in Poland,
January 1945. That season, snow
shuddered everywhere and ashes too descended
from crematoriums onto frozen glades.
The Turkish poet Nazim Hikmet wrote
to his wife from prison: *even at the dump*
our atoms will fall side by side.

Tired fires cleaved through cities, rivers
choked on human glands. Hemophilia wracked
von Hagens' childhood: blood scissored out
at every gust. Decades later, he invented
plastination to tame the rogue artery.
He became Doctor, curator of skulls,
Inventor, perfecter of preservation:
it takes three years to plastinate an elephant.
Two for a horse. Just one for a man.

III.

You, you are my clout, menagerie.
When I imagine your bedroom
positions, you will enact my fantasies.

In my dreams, I ask you to stop licking
your pelt, whip you like an elder god.
Your fats, sternums, orifices

will educate us, provide the jolt
for a Sunday afternoon. Soil
yourself and I'll be the one to wipe you,

I'll be the one to flense your skin.
Exhibit B: Chang and Eng, 1829.
Exhibit C: Afong Moy, 1834.

Exhibit D: Ota Benga, St. Louis
World Fair, 1904. It's a simple
exchange. We will pay for you.

Your hanging organs—our garden.
Gelatins astound us, fill us with relief
for what we have: golden hearts

that rouge the very air around.
Lungs that breathe. Gills that sing.
We are an abattoir of gratitude.

IV.

This is a fatty market. It blooms a corpulent
flower. Body suppliers. Rafflesia. Rapeseed. Boom,

boom, drones the Dalian corpse plant. Production
line: technicians dehydrate faces, bones, cartilage,

soak the cadavers in pink effluvia.
Autopsy hour—watch the fatty tissues sap,

seep, curdle. Watch the sticky plastic pump
into their ribs, ravish them. Kiss the cadaver

with a scalpel. Knives pare their eyes. Bad pears:
cores swarm with gnats, millipedes, wormseeds.

Insects coil over their golden flesh. Their
mouths are blood diamonds. Rumor has it,

the world is gorging on Chinese secrets.
Cover this wound before the flies find it.

V.

Sir, I look at you through your vitreous blue
eyes, and your shorn life passes through me
in one thrush. Boy who flunked his college

entrance exams. Man who ate abalone
from the can. How were you punished?
With bullwhips and jellyfish stings?

You died not long ago: I can tell by the way
your ligaments curl. Have you traveled
as far in your life as you've toured

posthumously, torqued in a prison
of cryogenic light? Amsterdam. Paris.
New York: what does it mean, anyway—

the provenance of a corpse? Who may possess
the body—spirit, demon, man, enter-
prise? You cannot exorcise the black

market from the body, though I want to smash
that slipshod glass, obliterate the price
on your head. I want to wreck the paraffin

that suspends your dancing spine in the air.
I scratch the cage, wipe your name
in pellucid bones. When they kick me

out, I search for you in my father's face
and find you in my son's. Pittsburgh's
highways soliloquize your anonymity,

your face on the billboard a marvel.
You gaze at my city with your pupils
sealed. Wherever I go now, you follow.

VI.

Thief of my skin, you can arrange my bones so I fly,
a raptor—you can cure my meat, summon the flies
in summer. My body is my crypt, your masterpiece.
Turkey vultures scare the stratosphere
searching for carrion, follow the scent in my limbs,
its feral suet. My name does not end in fury.
I'd rather you blow my alien bits into a black hole
than keep me here, intact and jaundiced. So please,
I ask: incinerate me. Let the sky be my open grave.

///   //   /

The Toll of the Sea

The first successful two-color (red and green) Technicolor feature, a retelling of *Madame Butterfly* starring Anna May Wong (1922)

GREEN means go, so run—now—

GREEN the color of *the siren sea, whose favors are a mortgage upon the soul*

RED means stop, before the cliffs jag downward

RED the color of the shore that welcomes

WHITE the color of the man washed ashore, from his shirt to his pants to his brittle shoes

WHITE the color of the screen before Technicolor

WHITE the color of the master narrative

GREEN the color of the ocean, so kind, not leaving a stain on the white shirt

GREEN the color of the girl, so kind—but why?

She speaks: *Alone in my garden I heard the cry of wind and wave*

In the green girl's garden, the stranger clamps her, asks:

How would you like to go to America?   A lie, soaked in the

RED of the chokecherries that turn brown in the heat

RED the color of the roses that spy

RED the color of their fake marriage

WHITE the color of the white man's frown

She asks: *Is it great lark or great sparrow you call those good times in America?*

GREEN the color of his departure

WHITE the color of the counterfeit letters she sends to herself

WHITE the color of their son

WHITE the color of erasure

RED the color of the lost footage

RED the sea that swallows our stories

RED the color of the girl who believed the roses

RED the color of the ocean that drowns the girl

RED the color of the final restoration

In every story, there is a Technicolor screen: black / white / red / green

In every story, there is a chance to restore the color

If we recover the flotsam, can we rewrite the script?

Alone in a stranger's garden, I run—I forge a desert with my own arms

BLUE the color of our recovered narrative

BLUE the color of *the siren sea*, which refuses to keep a white shirt spotless

BLUE the color of our reclaimed Pacific

BLUE the ocean that drowns the liars

BLUE the shore where the girl keeps living

There she rises, on the opposite shore

There she awakens—prismatic, childless, free—

Shorn of the story that keeps her kneeling

BLUE is the opposite of sacrifice

Anna May Wong on Silent Films

It is natural to live in an era
        when no one uttered—
and silence was glamour

so I could cast one glance westward
        and you'd know what I was
going to kill. Murder in my gaze,

treachery in my movements:
        if I bared the grooves
in my spine, made my lust known,

the reel would remind me
        that someone with my face
could never be loved.

How did you expect my characters
        to react? In so many shoots,
I was brandishing a dagger.

The narrative was enchanting
        enough to make me believe
I, too, could live in a white

palace, smell the odorless gardens,
        relieve myself on their white
petals. To be a star in Sun City—

to be first lady on the celluloid
        screen—I had to marry
my own cinematic death.

I never wept audibly—I saw my
        sisters in the sawmills,
reminded myself of my good luck.

Even the muzzle over my mouth
        could not kill me, though I
never slept soundly through the silence.

Anna May Wong Fans Her Time Machine

I've tried so hard to erase myself.
That iconography—my face
in Technicolor, the manta ray

eyelashes, the nacre and chignon.
I'll bet four limbs they'd cast me as another
Mongol slave. I will blow a hole

in the airwaves, duck lasers in my dugout.
I'm done kidding them. Today I fly
the hell out in my Chrono-Jet.

To the future, where I'm forgotten.
Where surely no one gives a fuck
who I kiss: man, woman, or goldfish.

In the blustering garden where I was fed
compliments like *you are our golden
apple* and *you are our yellow star*, I lost

my lust for luster. They'd smile, fuck
me over for someone else: ringletted women
with sloping eyelids played the Chinese

cynosure, every time. Ursa Minor, you never
warned me: all my life I've been minor,
played the strumpet, the starved one.

I was taproot and crook. How I've hunched
down low, wicked girl, until this good earth
swallowed me raw. Take me now, dear comet,

to the future, where surely I'll play
some girl from L.A., the unlikely heroine
who breaks up the brawl, saving everyone.

Anna May Wong Goes Home with Bruce Lee

We meet while he's filming *The Orphan*.
My young skin gleams. I'm in the future,
1960. My real self is alive somewhere,

but I've jinxed my own time machine to find
him. The bar sweats, sweet with salt, conk,
lacquer. The jukebox plays "Chain Gang."

We were born in the same golden state, surrounded
by cameras, chimeras for our other selves. He admits
some applause can be cruel, then steals a kiss.

Only he knows this terror—of casting so huge
a shadow over a million invisible faces. The silver
of our eyes dims them, and for that I don't forgive

myself. But Bruce understands. He knows the same
shame. On the dance floor, he cups the small
of my back, his hands cold like gauntlets.

I like how he describes a machete. How he hooks
his digits with my incisors, how he rips the skin
off bad memories, with just one lip, bloody apple,

and one battle has me pinned, saddled, on my spine.
In the aftermath, he reads me his poems—"Though
the Night Was Made for Loving" and "Walking along

the Bank of Lake Washington"—and kisses me
with both eyes open, staring straight into me.
At this time, my heart dead, little pigeon buried

beside the torn twig. He asks me to take him
with me, to the future. *It's the only place we can live
together*, he ventures. I want to say yes. I want to let

the flush flood us and take him there, our own
happy ending. But instead I say, *It's not ours to keep*.
Instead, I kiss him. I bury his silence with my mouth.

Anna May Wong Has Breakfast at Tiffany's

In Santa Monica, the sunrise has this way of emptying
everything inside you. I visit my future deathbed.
It's February 1961, and I watch myself sleep.

Dawn: outside my window, date palms sway and lovers
in blue Corvettes make their morning getaways.

There will never be another breakfast. I die of a heart
attack. Perhaps the night never pauses its seesaws.

Perhaps I resign myself: Holly Golightly, I can't go
lightly. I must face my fates—deception, despair, death.
Because being seen has a different meaning to someone

with my face. There will never be another breakfast.
The French toast sits untouched with the blackberries.

So I speed up time, reckless, toward a world
where I don't exist. Eight months later, Audrey Hepburn

walks down Fifth Avenue in a black Givenchy.
This is the role I'd have died for. This is love,
reciprocated. Beside her, Mickey Rooney plays Yunioshi,

another tapeworm-eyed uncle with a limp. And I yawn
at another generation of white men in yellowface.

Before him: Roland Winters, Sidney Toler, Warner Oland.
There is applause for them. The laughter is constant.
I have played their daughters—their pretty but untrustworthy

incarnates. There is no second generation for actors like me
but I've often pined for them. My progeny. Girls with tar-black
widow's peaks, who stumble across spotlights in purple tights,

taught to be meek. Girls who inherit my warnings, victories,
and failures, too. But for these girls, there will never be
breakfast. I will travel through all time searching for them.

Anna May Wong Blows Out Sixteen Candles

When I was sixteen, I modeled fur coats for a furrier.
White men gazed down my neck like wolves

but my mink collar protected me. When I was sixteen,
I was an extra in *A Tale of Two Worlds*. If I didn't pour

someone's tea, then I was someone's wife. Every brother,
father, or husband of mine was nefarious. They held me

at knifepoint, my neck in a chokehold. If they didn't murder
me, I died of an opium overdose. Now it's 1984

and another white girl awaits her sweet sixteen. It's 1984
and another white girl angsts about a jock who kisses

her at the end of the film. Now it's 1984 and Long
Duk Dong is the white girl's houseguest. He dances,

drunk, agog with gong sounds. All around the nation,
teens still taunt us. Hallways bloat with sweaters, slurs.

When I was eight, the boy who sat behind me brought pins
to class. "Do Asians feel pain the way we do?" he'd ask.

He'd stick the needles to the back of my neck until I winced.
I wore six wool coats so I wouldn't feel the sting. It's 1984

so cast me in a new role already. Cast me as a pothead,
an heiress, a gymnast, a queen. Cast me as a castaway in a city

without shores. Cast me as that girl who rivets center stage
or cast me away, into the blue where my lips don't touch

or say. If I take my time machine back to sixteen, or twenty,
or eight, I'd blow out all my candles. Sixteen wishes

extinguish and burn. The boy will never kiss me at the end
of the movie. The boy will only touch me with his needles.

/// // /

Antipode Essay

I. *Empire of Opposites*

Popular myth: if you dig a hole in the Montana badlands

through the earth's private parts,   your drill would end

up in China.   Maybe then you'd tear open the floor.

I was born   floating on a tendril of seaweed

and down the blue throat   of that hospital corridor,

you'd ride your drill   into a wall.

In that debris, consider: anti-ode,   antipode,

the geography of fallacies on which we build our empires.

II. *Terra Nullius*

America cannot orient
itself without an opposite.
What a shame its real antipode
is inhospitable ocean—all suds, spillage,

spume—archipelago, Kerguelen:
Desolation Islands, morphology
of volcanic flank, where I dream we crash-
land, lantanas shaking away

our grids and girdles. In this diurnal
romance, we feed the feral reindeer
all the food we have. Island scientists
launch rockets: *Centaure, Eridan,*

Super Arcas. Names for deserted
      myths. All winter we watch the sky grow
dim. Even Polaris cowers
      against the victrix of dawn.

III. *Terra Pericolosa*

When two poles oppose,
west is the center and the rest
a suspect terrain.

            Danger signs point at us. Unhook
            this vampire meridian—

hinterland of my blood,
      what's the antidote
for these boiling winters?

            For the heart's heavy skulking?

I don't blame
the ocean for
gorging on flotsam,
or eating people
alive.

IV. *Empire of Opposites*

In Bogota, on my knees
with altitude sickness. Through the hostel window,
constant lightning. All the ceiling beams gilded to Jakarta.

      Eyelids soldered
      to spoons, swooning temperature
      of the days.

I'll take back my hemisphere,
my haute other-hide. The longer I hide,
the brighter.

V. *Terra Incognita*

How democratic the stars were that night
the time we dug a hole

      to America. Little pennants
      announcing our penance
      for a youth misspent.

            Remember? It was December.
            Our train galloped by Beijing
            like a mare or its skeleton.

Through the window I saw
the city's dust lift the plenum
of black hair. *Where did our mettle
go*, someone asked, and I didn't know.

Metallurgy: in the antipode
of silence, we built platinum nests.

But here the earth
was wet with heliotrope
and the sorries
buried underneath
couldn't sprout.

If it rains enough, shame
may turn into seeds.

Close Encounters of the Liminal Kind

Maglev train, Beijing to Wuhan—
       snacks in the holster, I ride
the test track. We are crash test dummies

for levitation. Carry us, magnetic
       fields—marvel, our travel
at these speeds without wheels,

in the silver caul where we feel safe.
       I was born in Wuhan—left
at five, returning now. Here's my ticket,

stamped, ready, an apology
       for my foreign pelt. Childhood,
we used to sit three to one seat

as lightning poisoned the whole
       night white, and only sows
populated the passing cityscapes.

On the road, a man, two women
       and two children on their laps
cramp onto a single motorbike. Soil flies

beneath their heels. I watch them
       from my porthole, missing
wheels, missing motion, how it slices

softly, softly, to salvage friction
       against tracks, makes me think
of the homes I've lost to wilderness.

Someone says: *the invention*
        of speed will ruin us all.
Rails glisten like scriptures awaiting

translation. Someone stops reading
        his book and hurries toward
the exit. Someone gives up

his seat, drags his luggage
        across the platform. Someone
climbs quietly onto the tracks.

Sometimes I take weeks to remember
        a single word in my own tongue:
orange or *courage* or *please.*

Sometimes I take hours to work
        up the courage to ask a question.
This barreling quiet, our euphemism

for speed. Gone, ferromagnetic
        dreams—gone, fear of disquiet.
Once I met a boy on the overnight train.

I asked: *have you ever wondered*
        who walks across these fields
at night? Who has the nerve

to breathe that ghostly air? We snuck
        a kiss under his coat. Smoke
from other peoples' cigarettes

entered our bodies. Behind our faces,
        Wuhan scattered into fields
darkening with frost. This is a city

full of sensors. They detect
        the shapes of hips and mouths.
There is heat at the center of it.

Electronic Motherland

Foxconn Riots, Taiyuan, September 2012

Some nights I wish to see my mother this way: live, handheld,
                a breathing coma in my hands. Digit by digit my hand
comes apart, tissue from phalange, aluminum from bone.

An icepick for frost, a scalpel for lathe—I carve the icon
                into each metal press. Midnight in the dormitories: pigeons
drop shit on the suicide netting. Mysterious gods show me how

to replicate my hands, how to mold ammunition
                from shapeless muscle, how to play midwife to machines.
Each little wire insinuates our worth. Yesterday I obeyed,

but tonight we blow the bullhorn, trade our prowess
                for din. The factory's too quiet—it asks for siege. I love
a racket that kicks up dirt. It's our wager to march away.

The Mongolian Cow Sour Yogurt Super Voice Girl

Super girls drink melamine.
Melamine in scandalous milk

>   infects us / titillates us
>   until the red mouth bursts open
>   into a sewage of cherry petals.

Super girls, submit
your audition tapes: give us

>   your milky songs
>   sung in unmolested hours,
>   all the sad karaoke bars
>   in every spring city.

Sing, like sprained
finches, drive us mad with yearning
and dull the thrum of the mic.

>   Raise your shy voices, girls;
>   gorge on little gospels.

We'll toast to you, raise our glasses
to our lips, and quaff.

/ / /

Super girls wear iris-enlarging contacts
so the black universes of their pupils
sap all light. Touch every chandelier crystal.

Every camera flash enters. Their eyes stolen
like torn irises. I'm in the live audience
where they feed us live girls for supper.

The stage rinses us with its pulse. They step
out, broken hearts and all, warbling
for forgiveness. "Are you not my beloved?"

they ask, and we say *yes*, believing them.
Heat soaks our clavicles. Today I wave a torn
pennant for my sisters who stammer,

who get voted off stage, on fours before four
million, who wipe dirt off the altar of a cartoon
cow, for my sisters who float on eternal gondolas

drinking melamine from boxes, summer
wilting across their flat chests, their vocal
chords drowned in potable water.

/ / /

Super girls outperform their mothers.
Their mothers, of nondairy diets.
Their mothers, who snuck soy before dawn,

before the fields were razed, the time
when milk meant imperial muscles, thicker
hair, thighs, rounder infants. Their mothers

dreamt of dairy baths, curdling cheeses
out of reindeer milk, arms taut as Mongolian
nomads, wolf totems wishing for yogurt still.

So super girls were raised on dairy products
for their sinuous bodies. Super girls get epithetic
eye-fold surgeries. Give them your blessings,

mothers, even as the lighting smothers them.
Even if it pins them like flies to the territory
between camera and mouth. Where does flesh

end and fantasy begin? It's in the umber
that carves the fold above the eye, how it flutters
like mayflies in its mesh of nerve endings.

                    / / /

The camera pans to your vulnerable self.
The self you want to hide is a sad pretty thing
with spindles under its eyes. It has webbed

fingers. Out of its throat, a croak. Lashes plucked
from waterline, a moat of tears you hide
in your flask. Is this half-dead girl good to sing?

What do you say, lonely girl? What are you afraid of?
The audience is listening. Think on your feet,
now: what do you sing for? Go ahead: recite the list.

My ghost brother and sister. The vale where I was born
ashamed. My mother who gave me the milk
she couldn't drink. My bedridden story has yet to begin.

Electronic Necropolis

Guiyu Village, China

Behold how I tend to disappearance.
By slicing open dead circuitboards,
I cultivate rebirth. I douse
the hardware in pyretic acids
before it scrapes me, enters me, a lather of data
against my organs, bless them,
my warring insides. Even when the sun
half-drowns inside the black digital water,
its copper yoke doesn't reflect.
It is these nights that I get apprehensive:
the hard drives I'd gutted incant like ghosts—
oracular fossils that dream up other lives
as my family ails quiet over bitter melon soup.
Past supper we play cards, gamble away our scraps,
our sleep still short-circuiting.
In the lagoon a fish swims by, its scales
shooting jets of bitumen.
Amazing, such captivity; I can't help
marveling, as if I were on a plane going away
from Hong Kong, watching the city dismantle
beneath the fuselage—glowing, dying
circuit, ember half-faded into the skinless clouds.
What might—to shatter a microchip
with a pricked thumb. We unsolder our duress
with wire splinters, all lodged in our flesh
as if powering us. By noon, the megalomaniac
sun smiles down at the skinned machines.
It is the defects that incandesce, that supply
us with food, music, harm. The Lianjiang

River flows onward, north, toward the purple
rusk, the limestone cliffs. Under its water
skein, find the sum of foreign
dross. Riven, rising: a bloodless organ.

Riding Alone for Thousands of Miles

In Lijiang, the sign outside your hostel
        glares: Ride alone, ride alone, ride
alone—it taunts you for the mileage
        of your solitude, must be past

thousands, for you rode this plane
        alone, this train alone, you'll ride
this bus alone well into the summer night,
        well into the next hamlet, town,

city, the next century, as the trees twitch
        and the clouds wane and the tides
quiver and the galaxies tilt and the sun
        spins us another lonely cycle, you'll

wonder if this compass will ever change.
        The sun doesn't need more heat,
so why should you? The trees don't need
        to be close, so why should you?

The sea is full of jetsam tonight. A thousand
        miles away, you think of shores,
sitting at the KTV bar in Lijiang, listening.
        A song comes up: Jay-Z with Rihanna,
        umbrella-ella-ella-eh, strangers singing
into the strange night, and it's like home to you,
        this cocktail of ashes dusting your knees.
This city is famous for yak meat, rhododendron,
        and one-night stands. You wait for yours
to show up. He works at the bar, looks like Takeshi
        Kaneshiro. He clutches your waist as you ask
        for more songs, more wine, more fruit.
Another: Teresa Teng, whose voice is the song
        you have in common. "The Moon Represents
        My Heart"—but tonight the moon represents
        your sorrow in the Old Town Square.
Later as you lie in the cheap hotel in the electric
        New City, Takeshi tells you he has never
        left this province his whole life.
His family grows a peach orchard, and the fattest
        peaches ripen in September. *Where can I mail
you a peach?* he asks. Tell him you're flying
        to Indonesia. He asks why you're going
somewhere so far away. Say: in Manhattan,
        there are thousands of gargoyles
        that travel around the world
        as everyone else sleeps.
Say: in Brooklyn, there is a chance
        to rebuild a life from trash—
        long-stemmed roses blooming
in the dumpsters, bodegas spilling purple
        dragonfruit still good to eat.
Say: one morning outside Bryant Park,
        you stood watching a garbage

fire destroy a basket of rotten mangoes.
    Within five minutes, firefighters
came to extinguish it. You peered inside
        afterward, and the nothing you saw
        was wet and dark and smoldering.
Above you, a crane lifted a tiny man higher
        and higher, until light stretched
        his limbs into a sheaf of minerals.
He was dust before the wrecking
        ball swung.

This land promises snowfall. This land promises windfall.
This land promises the return of brief days. May this land
promise you a body, some muscle, some organ, a brain.

Some ribs made of dark tinder, their insides lit, all vesicle,
atrium. May this kindling promise you a hearth and last

past your dread, October's sleet, past scarred trees, then winter,
then mend and on and onward and orbit you so you are blank
as memory, turn into paper—crinkle, burn, and finally open.

The Diary of Afong Moy

No. 8 Park Place, Manhattan, November 1834

The merchant brothers who brought me here,
      Freddy and Nate Carne, knew I'd make
it rain for them. In their eyes I was a hothouse
      flower, a goddess of $$$$$$$$$$$$$$.
They decorated me with precious imports—
      baubles, yellow pantalettes, damasks—
then placed me in a diorama of snuff boxes
      and silk. I was a breathing mannequin
on my brocade throne. I couldn't believe how
      many people paid to see me. Banknotes
dropped, jawbones dropped, and it was truly
      unnerving, to watch the white people
stare at me, mouths twitching in awe or pity,
      or both. The men looked at my little
feet. The women, at my regalia. They wanted
      to see my feet uncovered, can you believe
the nerve? The podiatrists, the reporters, begged
      for a glimpse. At the men, I snickered.
At the women, I smiled. They swooned, blushed,
      as if they swallowed Sichuan peppercorns.
Their corsets were killing them.
      Heavens! A grotesquerie, their spines
all crooked in their skeletons. I raised my brows,
      ensconced in my civilized box.
I counted the days with my abacus.
      Look, I was fucking
      bored. Was I the animal here? Or were they?
On my throne in lonely New York, I presaged
my own descent. It began with a tongue, English

creature, that curled its way into my mouth.
They called me the Celestial Princess. I wanted
        them to bow down. So they did—they fell
at my feet in penance. Or worship. A vernissage
        of my ancestors across my face. A slap.

The Oval Office, Washington, D.C., 1835

They took me to the capital.
        Winter, gray as steel,
the White House, with its forlorn arches.
        Give me a coronation,
a title: queen of a bastardized

empire. Let me quench America's
        thirst for royalty. I performed
a song in Cantonese for the President
        of the United States
of America, Mr. Andrew S. Jackson.

Glory is a strange concept here—
        No riches, no throne,
no robes, no royalty. He seemed
        polite enough, but he was no
emperor. Atung warned me:
        don't get too confident.

Mr. President may look unremarkable,
        but beneath his skin, lodged
near his heart, are bullets never removed
        from when he murdered
a man. This nice man is a slave
        trader, plantation owner,
founder of the Democratic Party,
        and his nickname? Jackass.

Mr. President shook my hand, stared
        at my feet like other men,
begged me to ask my countrymen
        to change their laws.

I sang. I hollered. My whole
life in my throat. To the audience,
        my voice sounded ghastly,
my words were inscrutable.

        The lyrics, if I remember—
how a face conceals its intentions
        like a woman conceals her name.

Charleston, South Carolina, 1835

Antebellum South blew a breeze through my skull
        like something hot and rotting.
        In Charleston, the public
        began demanding me to strip.

Take off your shoes, they said. They wanted my naked
        feet, and even I barely saw my own feet
        uncovered. And then they took my shoes
        off, one by one, the skin underneath
        glowing translucent. They loved how I
        flinched, my cheeks burning like copper.

By evening, the muskets sounded off, the riots
        blasted, screams all night. Rebellion
        painting the towns all ghostly. Something
        in me stole away, ran for the hills covered
        in mist, ran for the sea. In the end
        my diorama was a diorama, not a house
        with a roof. It wasn't fireproof.

In my Southern sleeping chambers, I dreamt
        of home—the fishing village, the locust
        tree near the river where I used to sit
        with friends. My father in the foyer,
        counting coins, scraping rice in his bowl.
        A silver spoon is an American import,
        the only one he could trade for tea.

But I was his biggest Canton export, a living
        specimen. A button-eyed doll. My eyes
        could see the specters in their cities,
        my nose could smell the murders
        in their field, my ears could hear
        the clamors in their forest, and at last

I lost it; I smashed the trinkets. Snuffed
        the snuff boxes, tore the silk, raided
        the chests, drank all the wine, ripped
        the irises from their parched soil. Panic
        plundered the property! Its wreckage
        was my greatest show on earth—

The Barnum Years, 1844—?

The show must go on. And on and on,
        replaced by another show, and that's the trouble
with artifice. It never ends. Mr. Phineas T. Barnum
        loved his freaks, a prophet for profits, from ersatz
mermaid to Giantess to Joice Heth, her frail immortality.

        In the newspaper he questioned whether I'd ever
been a *Lady*. Brought another family of Celestials,
        advertised their veracity to discredit me.
As if there couldn't be two respectable Chinese ladies
        in America at the same time. To promote

one, strip the dignity of the other. There was no word
        for tokenism in those days of yore.
When you were rare, when you were a Lady,
        you had to be tender, you had to be good.

///   //   /

Anna May Wong Meets Josephine Baker

Casino de Paris, seat in the back. It's 1932 and I'm in exile

again. Paris makes the best kind of exile—the woman on stage

agrees, riding in on her mane of sequined feathers. Horses

like white phantoms galloping under her dress. What is it

about the stage lights that casts our bodies both desirable

and diabolical? She lifts her wings, and air rushes—lightning

strikes the audience, the white feathers fall. I catch her eye

at midnight and she invites me into her dressing room. Blood

orange peels scatter on the ground. Her cockatoos wail

in a cage, her pet cheetah spread-eagled on her alpaca furs.

We toast to *Piccadilly*, Paris, drink brandy, chat about home—

all the reasons we left, all the reasons we're homesick still.

The first time I left, I watched the Statue of Liberty vanish

into a bloodless mile of water. I didn't expect I would feel

nothing, Josephine says. *The arrival, by comparison, fueled*

this frenzy, this fire in me. There is no feeling like clenching a new country's soil in your fist, then washing it off with a new

country's soaps. The fall we were both in Berlin, the image

Paul Colin painted of her graced all the rainy street signs:

La Revue Nègre Champs-Elysées, Le Tumulte Noir 1929.

I saw her at the German salons Marlene Dietrich took me.

Marlene watched her, as everyone watched her—the lick

of hair, her arms moving like steam engines. Perhaps

we even danced together, beaded skirts hiked to knees,

the Charleston in the empty predawn hours, bowls shattering,

chandeliers dropping their crystals, until security hurled

us outside and we laughed in the face of this exile,

the Indian summer warmth sloughing all the dead weight

away. It was a life worth abandoning anything for.

I left home because I dreaded how that screen disfigured me.

Though I don't completely escape it here, Josephine says.

I want to tell her about my time machine. I want to say:

We don't have to stay here, in this time and space,

where we are carrion pecked at by flaneurs *and crows.* Triple

leavetaking—body, birthplace, adopted home—Santa Monica

and St. Louis, New York, Berlin, Paris—we were born

to beg and bow in this country. So Josephine left, searching

for another exit, one without Jim Crow's hoofprint

on every cinema, restaurant, door. We had to prove

ourselves *different*: our limbs, dancing, trained like racehorses,

bred, polished, for what? In the end, we still pined for shelter.

In the end, we still guarded our bones against the blaring thunder.

Anna May Wong Makes Cameos

Romeo Must Die (2000): I'm Aaliyah's
      sassy friend. I give her tough love
      and good advice. *Kiss Jet Li*, I tell her.
      The director cuts their kissing scene,
      replaces it with a hug,
      rendering my scene pointless
      so they cut me from the film.

Kill Bill (2003): I'm Gogo Yubari's
      grieving twin sister. In my nightmares,
      Chiaki Kuriyama swings her iron balls
      over my futon. The noise maddens me.
      To avenge her, I lunge with a steak knife
      at Uma's white veil. I die as my bones
      crunch under her heels.

The Last Samurai (2003): I'm Tom Cruise's
      love interest's younger cousin.
      So frail I cry at the sound of a twig
      cracking. In the end I am sacrificed
      so Tom can shed tears—take comfort
      in my pretty cousin as my spine goes limp.

"Hollaback Girl" (2004): I'm Gwen Stefani's
      archnemesis: the cute Asian
      girl who disses her behind
      the school bleachers. Once I was
      her backup minion. Now no more—
      I've gone rogue. Pharrell is the other
      cameo. Together we conspire to take
      her down. There are claws. There is gore.

In the end, the showdown is cut
to make room for Gwen's cheerleading routine.

Memoirs of a Geisha (2005): I'm Gong Li's
        evil apprentice geisha. I trip young Sayuri
        with my silk sash. I set her kimono on fire.
        The rival okiya crackles, burns. As the beams
        fall down in ashes, lightning whips the howling
        door. Dew drips down my forehead, my jewels.
        In the confusion, I perish, of course.

Anna May Wong Rates the Runway

Even the white models
all wear their hair in straight bangs.
The Asian models, too—like clones

they glide out, lush throats
throttled by nephrite. The editors
call the pieces "1920s chinoiserie."

I call them glorified dog collars.
One by one they strut, chameleons,
fishnetted darlings with red lips

that imply: diablerie. These women
slip into the diabolical roles
I've played but don't pay for it.

Now I am someone's muse.
Good. It's February, Fashion Week.
The coldest winter since weather

went live. Everywhere still—pale
legs exposed to infernal snow.
I want to trust the mohair

to keep me warm—I want to trust
the cloth that holds me close.
But in this room, the spotlight flatters

every flaw. When the show is over,
the applause is meant for stars
but my ovation is for the shadows.

Anna May Wong Dreams of Wong Kar-Wai

I know what it is to pretend to be safe
in my fulvous skin. So much pretending
can bring a girl to her knees.

But in Wong Kar-Wai's world, no one
needs to pretend. The mise-en-scene
of *Fallen Angels*: Hong Kong trance,

butcher's storefronts, stolen ice cream
trucks. Or *2046*: the train of lush cyborgs
going forever nowhere. In the Singapore

hotel room, Tony Leung writes his alien
love stories. Across the world, *Happy Together*:
Leslie Cheung empties his apartment

in Buenos Aires. Sets for the beautiful
and lonely. In *Chungking Express*, I watch
Faye Wong smoke cigarettes between takes

in cropped cut, oversized button-down, grosgrain
shorts. She doesn't leave her tape deck alone,
but complains she is sick of that track,

"California Dreamin'." The song makes
me homesick, nostalgic even, and I know
this is absurd because it came out in 1965,

after I die. Whatever John Phillips meant
by feeling safe in L.A., I can relate.
Sometimes I pretend so much I believe

myself. On the set, I try on the yellow wig
and trenchcoat that Bridgette Lin wore
smuggling cocaine in the first act.

The plot has a hole: why does Bridgette wear
a blonde wig, if she didn't want to arouse
suspicion? I have played many criminals,

but no one like her, who fell asleep
in a hotel room with the police officer
gazing at her, in love. If I played her role,

I imagine walking through Causeway Bay
in 1929, my cigarette lighting my way,
the most conspicuous woman in the world.

But the role I'd rather play is Faye's:
tomboy who breaks into her true love's
apartment to add goldfish to his fishtank.

Or Agent, in *Fallen Angels*, who sets up crime
scenes and goes to her assassin's room
to touch herself. Or Maggie Cheung's role

in *Days of Being Wild*: she asks the traitor
in her bed, does the empty night fertilize
this barren soil? She is ruddy in pale light,

limp with the pain of wakefulness. Far away,
the palm trees flare over wet boughs. Home
is in Macau. The rain readies her for her dim

walk home. I've never cared for love stories.
I praise a story of heartbreak. I praise
how beauty looks during a blackout.

Anna May Wong Stars as Cyborg #86

The future is as sterile as a robot's loincloth.
I drown my hands in sanitizer until they pucker.

Where this soapbox tree germinates, I collect
my germs and make a fountain of them.

Because yellow is yarrow and soot, and the future,
I've learned, is no suture. Because where I'm from,
these kisses are infections. Because dirt's

ammunition against discipline, the blood fills
my clean mouth with dismay. Am I surprised—
Hollywood still assumes we are all the bastard

children of the same evil dictator? That phosgene
and mustard will rack our titanium Maoist husks
until some white man with slanty eyes rescues us

from our mealy, pliant selves? Am I to wear Dior,
wrap my mouth in bloody tulle, before kneeling,
bending to kiss a mouth dirtied by Pantone 136?

No fucking thanks. Because where I'm from,
these kisses are infractions. Darlings, let's rewrite
the script. Let's hijack the narrative, steer

the story ourselves. There'd be a heist, a battle.
Audre Lorde would write the script. My leading
man would be Bruce. We'd earn our happy ending.

Instead, they give me 1981. 2012. Quantum quasars,
new dystopia—plutonium wars. We're not in Polanski's
Chinatown anymore. Yet we still have the same bowl

haircuts. Bangs, big bang, a city of fetid promise, new
minor galaxy where we cannot touch. Instead our skin
is rust and metal. It gratifies the technophile in all of us.

Anna May Wong Goes Viral

In the future, there's an oracle
        where you can search
for where you belong. I ask this engine
        and it replies:
do the deleted scenes choke you
        up? In the future, I am young
and poor, so I become a webcam girl.

On camera I read passages
        from Russian novels.
Curious netizens subscribe to my site
        then cancel, ranting on forums
about my prudish act, how no one wants
        to see a girl bend over
a thick book and wheeze.

After I go viral, I shut down my website.
        Screenshots circulate cyberspace—
Anna, dressed as a purple panda,
        Anna, taking a swig from a demitasse.

I collect all the passwords to my shrines.
        I hack into them, grow a habit
of Photoshopping hyena spots onto
        my own skin and uploading
my spoiled face onto Instagram.

My complexion has the mottle
        of century eggs. My mustaches grow
feather tufts. I replace the paillettes
        on my gowns with scales.

Recently, on the red carpet, I wear dresses
        made of kelp, breathe
through fake gills and carry plastic
        sacs full of saltwater.

Soon a crop of young girls will join me,
        renouncing their dresses to wade
in the thrill of being animal.

/// // /

Ghost in the Shell

In late summer's cyberpunk heaven,
        I wake up with a different face.

Who am I? Champion of drowning,
        champion of loss—do I dare proclaim,
with a cyborg body, this humanity is my own?

My name is Motoko Kusanagi, investigator
        cyborg for Public Security Section 9,
reporting a cyberterrorist crime. Year 2017:

someone has implanted Scarlett Johansson's
        face onto mine, hacked my ghost, installed
an imposter's memories, reprogrammed

my optic nerves, diluted my brain into a white
        projection. A Thermo-Optical camouflage
gone haywire, a rogue scrim for my body
        that is not my body—I am now a double,

a replicant, an agent of carnage. Hacker,
        Puppet Master of the laws that govern film—
let this message be clear: *I do not comply.*

You can bedevil me with fabrication, but I
        transmit the truth. It's in the data, the stars,
my blood, my spit, my wires, my parts. God

as my witness, I, Motoko, will self-destruct
        this celluloid screen. So watch out, Scarlett
O'Hara, this brutish reign of cinematography
        is about to end—history flensed, data wiped.

Flesh precedes computers, sweat precedes data.
　　　Before everything was stolen, our lives were ours.

Let's be gentle with each other in this new
　　　megalopolis. The sun doesn't set in *Lost*
in Translation, but I will make sure it does here.

Dirge with Cutlery and Furs

> I'm usually very miserable,
> so I buy a fur coat every year.
> —*Daul Kim, 1989–2009*

When you died, I felt like kissing
a pencil and breaking it into pieces
eating it stuffed inside a spring roll
with enough ginger to make my nose snot
and it wasn't because I knew you or coveted
your leathers: it was because you collected
forks and read Tolstoy on the toilet
seat in Paris, because you loved guinea
pigs and smiled on the Anna Sui
runway when you weren't supposed to,
and for that I, too, like to fork myself—
you, who bought the pants off a homeless
man and wore them, who pretended
you were a monster with your paillettes
on macramé, your face paler than the flesh
of a nashi pear. What was this wish for the hour
when no one sees her face on the spoon?
Say hi to your warmest destination: not sauna,
nor tropics, nor lovers—it was the heat source
in the furs—capybara furs, flame-retardant
furs, furs knives couldn't cut, furs that trapped
oxygen, human body, and you, swimming
now, out at sea in your midnight flowers,
Angora rabbits, where the monsters
stay lovely every fall and spring.

Yume Miru Kikai [The Dreaming Machine]

After Satoshi Kon, with lines borrowed from Satoshi Kon's
last letter, translated by Makiko Itoh

1. The impulse to have heart is the engine propelling us nowhere.

2. The Dreaming Machine predicts the past. The Dreaming Machine remembers
    the future.

3. Kon: transfiguration. Epochs, seasons, mise-en-scènes turn like weather vanes,
    but a single desire stays immutable.

4. In *Millennium Actress*, Chiyoko runs through flying snow. Hokkaido's land-
    scape burns her lungs. She veers toward the train station, plummets down a hill
    crawling with bugs and cherry blossoms.

5. In *Tokyo Godfathers*, the cardboard homes of the homeless are more inviting
    than the derelict homes of the blessed.

6. *How to live your life in a world that gets so stupefying?* Kon asked once in an
    interview.

7. The Dreaming Machine is vanishing, flashing like the teeth of the city you
    bypass on a plane to an unfathomable town.

8. In the preliminary sketches, three robots go on an adventure to a humanless
    multiverse.

9. Shot #1: girl robot nurses heart machine with sparkplug.

10. *July the 7th. It was a rather brutal Tanabata . . .*

11. 2010: Satoshi lies on a bed, dreaming of dreaming machines. The rest of his life stares back in the five feet before him.

12. Always the question: is nowhere as unknown as we have feared? How will we brave this antimatter?

13. Hurting, hurling, hurtling—

14. Toward heaven. Fulfillment of what? May harbors, our heads on the laps of our springtime lovers . . .

15. Tanabata: a broken tree harbors wishes. On July 7th, 2007, I held one of these broken wishes to my chest as Yokohama's harbors flared with drifting ships.

16. Where do you wander, where do you search for this petal that grows from the stone in your chest?

17. *And, if I may ask you for one more thing—could you help my wife send me over to the other side after my death? I'd be able to get on that flight with my mind at rest if you could do that for me. I ask this from my heart.*

18. Flight: the dreaming machine flies into the ruined city. All the computers sing. The circuits light up like fireworks.

19. Devastation: the temple painted gold. Devastation: the aftershocks of a prediction come true.

20. Shot #2: robot beholds a golden city that waits beyond the gateway. City ruined by its beauty—the tidal epochs hunt the domes.

21. On someone's bed, I read Satoshi's last letter. It was June. I was between apartments. A heat wave plowed through Brooklyn. My breath was summer's jailbird. A beautiful man lay beside me, unmoved. His perfect ribs did not shake. This is how I knew to go.

22. Now the stolen gospels unwind. Now the blueprint disappears.

23. *With my heart full of gratitude for everything good in the world, I'll put down my pen. Now excuse me, I have to go.*

24. The robot crosses the threshold, enters the ruined city. Spires gleam like crypts before him.

25. *The Dreaming Machine*'s website is defunct. 600 shots made; 900 to go.

26. Eerie suspension—a dreaming machine floats like a gondola on a blue lake. Mist covers his circuits, protects him. A dreaming machine flashes in the teleprompter.

27. When are you naked if you are a robot? Answer: when your circuits are exposed, your dreams open to hacking. Paprika knows this.

28. Three dreaming machines meet in an unknown future. Overhead, the meteors stop to listen, but in a moment desert us again.

The Five Faces of Faye Valentine

After Cowboy Bebop

One: her battle face is indistinguishable
        from her poker face. No savant dares
        to romance a face like that. Eyebrows, smirk,
        her mouth a lawless husk. Master swindlers
        beware: she will one-up you with a flawless
        feint. A fugitive wind shrouds her name,
        her debt. There's a bounty on her swagger.

Two: girl. Orphanage. Accident. Cryogenic sleep.
        Black dog serenades rouse her from tides.
        She doesn't recognize the child on the beta
        tapes—purple hair, white ribbons tying
        her features together. Jupiter jazz crows,
        her childhood, sleep until the earth disappears.

Three: woman. Always running. Always running
        out of fuel. Always straddling a slow horse,
        Red Tail, stranded in space with an unloaded
        pistol. This is what night imagined when it imagined
        a feral woman, jaw open and swiping. Windward.
        Loose claw. Less sigh than scowl. The last civet
        in the universe gnashes her teeth against the glass.

Four: questioning. Is there mercy for a mercenary
        out there in the writhing galaxy,
        where jetties disappear into harbors
        drained of antimatter? Bounty hunters
        lurk in the undertow. Evening larks afoot.

Five: conquest. Here's her blackjack. Her torn
    jacket, her din, her turn. Her ammunition,
    her departure. Unrecognizable cities rise
    from empty shuttles, husks for drones.
    See you space cowboy, screams the Callisto
    Moon. On nights when the wind strips
    the highway bare, only the stars hunt her down.

Lavender Town

Don't let the sour flowers fool you, child.

This town is a dead town. The tower tolls
              to your trill, your heartbeat,
              inaudible
to everyone except you.   You listen. You hear.
              Ghost notes, discordant leaves
clutter the earth, tin and rustle—
              a lachrymose bird cries,
a graveyard glistens. When you climb the stairway,
              don't shield your eyes
              from the pixels, 30 hertz heat—
don't shield your awe
              from the ghosts of pretty prey.
The ones you catch
              when you're alone and afraid.

Lavender Town, noble purple town, plumed, perfumed
              dream of violet fields—can you hear
the killing machine sing? What secrets hide?
              Why run?   Why hold on?
You walk by the side of the road, biting an apple
              as you wave your thumb—
              blood sickles down, a rebel
you are, a hitchhiker, a tiny savant.

When you grow up, and the screen lights up
              all your blind
              spots, and you replace the dead
green cartridge
              with a blank one of your making,

you'll arrive, at last, at the final
                battle. Maybe then you'll find
                that the game you're playing
is a hack—you thought you were invincible,
                and just like that, the boss
KOs you. And other times, you're astonished
                at your own breath.
Other times, you thought you were dead,
                but your body was eternal all along.

The Death of Ruan Lingyu

Shanghai, 1935

In your role for *New Women*, you played Wei Ming,

a single mother, novelist, who dies as she declares

she wants to live. In your dream, Wei Ming lived,

kneeling at her daughter's grave. You reach through

the celluloid to try and touch her, but the screen turns

dark, then bright with waves. Interrogate the Suzhou River:

why drown the shore? Why? Entire shorelines of new women

surge, ebb, turn to foam. You see their limbs in the water,

thrashing, with nowhere to go. You can't save

them, touch them, make their feral grief any more

endurable. Instead, they vanish. Instead, they recede.

Laundry baskets scatter, upturned, laundry piles

on the rooftops, laundry in the snow. You subsist on spit,

spite, spotlight. You subsist on fright, moving

across your face like a freight train over frozen tracks.

Who carries you across the four-poster bed, the medicine

cabinet, the pot of porridge? All you wanted was the lie

where the beautiful disobedient ones survive.

Soon their absence becomes your own. Your cigarette

lights the frigid air, burning a hole in the landscape.

After Nam June Paik

Good Morning Mr. Orwell (1984)

We wake up to the era of a doom tube. Save
        us, save us, save us—if our suffering

        is broadcasted, let it be known.
Let it be collective. Let it be real, let it be
        the future real soon.

Opera of our nightmares, today is the day
        the heavens have promised: the day we survive

ourselves, move forward and fast. Farther and farther
        the sky rumbles over us—faster and faster,

the transmissions, boomtowns, bodies in space:
        New York to Paris, Berlin to Seoul, WNET

to Centre Pompidou, we broadcast
        our triplicate shadows, our robot politics,

we install our souls, our space yodels, our rebel kisses,
        into your television set, your cell phones,

until the moon rises
                in your kingdom
      and drowns in the cove of our satellite waves.

Opera Sextronique

> "In my videotaped electro-vision, not only do
> you see your picture instantaneously and find
> out what kind of bad habits you have, but see
> yourself deformed in twelve ways."
>
> —*Nam June Paik*

12 ways I see myself deformed—

1)   shower: behind the fog, water, chemicals, dye, I die
        like suds, slip down the drain. I die like my own cells
        to clean my whole self.   if this really meant rebirth.
        if this really meant change.   or growth or vanishing.

2)   2 movements: sprinting to fulton street, the A or G, nostrand, bedford
        hair all static electricity skull all circuitboard—
        the windows on the trains like touchscreens
        through which we breathe our anonymous breath.

3)   subsistence on absence, or subsistence on substitutes.
        substitute part of a substitute whole.

                          we are all your substitute holes.

4)   staring at myself in a mirror inside another mirror, entering these mirrors,
        accidentally scraping myself with these mirrors, touching myself
        through these mirrors, a labyrinth of mirrors, a language of mirrors,
        a labyrinth of chaos, yellow finches, finding no exit,
        and there is no exit from the labyrinth of mirrors.

5)   canceled TV show: errant body cloaked in wires.
        TV bra, TV cello, static, concerto, radio silence, rainbow
        of a lost transmission.
        your body is my search engine.
        I want to question it.

6)   on the LCD screen, I offer light but no breath.
        I author breadth but no depth.
        catch me drawing a portrait of these deformities
        on my tablet with my guilty fingerprints.
        catch me   drawing you.
        to say I miss you: I can't. my phone has buried my mouth.
        I am afraid of instant messages. most times it's unbearable.
        I prefer the slow, gradual ones.

7)   sex is the pulse of a burning screen wrapped around your body. sex is the living
        sculpture. with this video monitor appendage, you are a minotaur, buff
        and brief. the video bra cages your breasts. the video penis makes you a machine.
        monitor lizards crawl over the powerpoints.

8)   then the bit about repulsion: about the monstrous static of sexual scripts.
        I don't remember submitting to that. I sit with a man at a café table in central park.
        he doesn't see my story. he threshes it, bends it, sucks it in like a vampire.
        pretty girls and money, the trouble with loneliness.
        always the ugly suits, fingernail clippings. thirsty mouths.
        I don't remember tasting this tongue like a dead fish inside my mouth,
        closing my eyes, scalding.

9)   utopian laser TV station: I record myself reborn. I record myself unborn.
        I record myself a stillbirth.

10)   (absence)   plant your nightmares in the soil / plant your wounds in the dirt

11)   (rebirth)   they sprout into birds of paradise / they sprout into trees

12)   love is the refraction, pellucid as bone. if I can locate the gleam on the other side of
       the planet. the one who sees me whole. the one who honors my narrative,
       does not bend it, thresh it, obstruct or smash it. this I yearn. if I could plug my
       senses into that socket. let there be light.

Li Tai Po

After Li Po and Janelle Monáe

You, robot-poet, hold four texts: pretext, subtext,
        context, metatext.

O hexarchy of dead kings, the Monarch seat is empty.
        I can't see much through this stereoscope: only frozen
earth. A tundra, a wasteland, an orchard of scorched trees.

        I wait for your poems, like baroque lasers.
I bring you offerings: yuzu, pear, mission fig.

Dear robot, dear poet: I long to meet you in a new world
        where we can live our midsummer's cyberpunk dream.
Can we write this text together, rewrite history, rewrite his story,
        sneak past the auditorium of ruins—

your body of ten antique TV cabinets: antique radio cabinet / Korean printing block
        Korean palimpsest / eleven color televisions

Let's recite a cento: Before my bed, the moon is shining bright,
                            We suffered a rare, rare blue
                            I think that it is frost upon the ground.
                            So much hurt / I raise my head and look at the bright moon
                            On this earth / I lower my head and think of home.

Or two: Into a valley of a thousand bright flowers,
                            all the birds and the bees, dancing with the freaks in the trees,
                            watch the water turn to wine
                            with the willow-flakes, falling like snow, and the vermilion

girls getting drunk about sunset
outer space and out your mind
and the waters, a hundred feet deep reflecting green eyebrows
Will you be electric sheep, electric ladies, will you sleep?
There is no end of things in the heart.

My robot, my poet, ancient and erstwhile and now
        and f—ever,
the best mischief: to be stranded in this electricity with you.

Mall of the Electronic Superhighway

travelers in the night, united states of wanderers—

welcome to the fluxus department store, your end of the world stop for your road trip
      you can wander these future stalls, where our hungry souls touch each other
      you can buy makeup made of mica, android pixels, space vectors, HD display:
      transform your face into a glowing orb
      transform your face into a projection of the night

mall of the universe, mall of the multiverse, mall of wave-function collapse—
      you can meet and greet with the holographic dead.
      read james baldwin at the mall, he comes to life and whispers:
            "the old survivals of my generation will be wiped out.
            western civilization is heading for an apocalypse."
      if this doesn't comfort you, whitney, michael, and prince
      will sing in your ear. you will weep together. you will not be alone.

it really is a miracle—that the electronic mall can curate an apocalypse
      into a beautiful, fashionable memory the texture of the silk
      you can't afford.

in 2005, a year before nam june paik died, the biggest mall in the world
      was built in dongba, china, and now it is an empty megalopolis,
      all the storefronts foreclosed, ghosts of dead enterprises
      rippling the manmade dam. no one operates the machinery.
      once I fell in love in an empty mall.
      twice I fell in love in an empty parking lot.

the surveillance camera records our prettiest nightmares. silkscreen >
      touchscreen > monitor screen > tv screen. dreams whose warm
      light baptizes you. disbelief, disappear.
      go ahead: believe in miracles. believe in beauty and the universe and the future.

our gear will transport you when you're sleeping. somnambulating shoes
so your body doesn't have to.

sprint a thousand miles in your future kicks, alison brand atom shoes.
    ditch your car in a ditch, with its sad steering wheel, its sad locomotion.
    you can travel from harlem to wall street in fifteen minutes with these tiny
    atomic engines. you can be naked in the city, and no one
    will see you through how fast you're flying.

The Death of Robot K-456

The robot opera sends us to space.
We look down. We don't miss our lovers.
Instead, we're nostalgic for gravity.

Permutations of ground: cement,
grass, parquet, soil. Premonitions
of sound: crash, pow, shriek.

Down on earth, we saw the tragedy—
the machine cracked under slow wheels.
His cords and his bowels, twitching.

The machine defecated on itself,
spilling all its beans. We looked away.
In another time, we would mourn.

But for now, we hover, above patrols,
above surveillance, above the borders,
like migrants to a black hole, a Xanadu

where no one dreams of finding us.
Even if we cut off a limb or leap over
an edge, no eyes watch us. We are free.

Oculus

After Solange, "An Ode To"

May. Pale peonies on the sills.
    From the steps of the New York Public Library,
        we hailed a taxi uptown, past the lions—
            past Patience,
                past Fortitude,
        to the Guggenheim, where we sat, lotus
        style, wearing head-to-toe white
with a sea of others.

They checked our phones and cameras at the door.
    All of us, a cloud condensing
        into ourselves. Our forms.
            All city, all air, all sugar, all brown,
      all gold—have a seat,
this is a cause for celebration.

In many places in the world, it could have been
    a funeral. She appeared and she sang,
            descending down the spirals,
      the golden nautilus—past
    the skeletal Giacomettis, past the Duchamps,
past the Modiglianis, under the centripetal glass—

a single layer in the interior. None of our names
    were there. But our bodies. There they were.
        The most photographed place on earth
           was where we sat
        without cameras
except our eyes and our faces.

It was spring. I was still hopeful. In my chest, what beat
            was cracked but still salvageable. Cherry petals
                  strewing my shoulders, a whir. Cranes
            in the sky, cranes threaded on my dress.
                  Golden tubas warbled
      as she danced. We looked up, and there was

            a skylight, a dome—the oculus
at the center, through which all fears still burned
            and awed.

///   //   /

Resurrection

In the autumn I moved to New York,
I recognized her face all over the subway
stations—pearls around her throat, she poses
for her immigration papers. In 1924, the only
Americans required to carry identity cards
were ethnically Chinese—the first photo IDs,
red targets on the head of every man, woman,
child, infant, movie star. Like pallbearers,
they lined up to get their pictures taken: full-face
view, direct camera gaze, no smiles, ears showing,
in silver gelatin. A rogue's gallery of Chinese
exclusion. The subway poster doesn't name
her—though it does mention her ethnicity,
and the name of the New-York Historical
Society exhibition: *Exclusion/Inclusion.*
Soon, when I felt alone in this city, her face
would peer at me from behind seats, turnstiles,
heads, and headphones, and I swear she wore
a smile only I could see. Sometimes my face
aligned with hers, and we would rush past
the bewildered lives before us—hers, gone
the year my mother was born, and mine,
a belt of ghosts trailing after my scent.
In the same aboveground train, in the same
city where slain umbrellas travel across
the Hudson River, we live and live.
I've left my landline so ghosts can't dial me
at midnight with the hunger of hunters
anymore. I'm so hungry I gnaw at light.
It tunnels from the shadows, an exhausting
hope. I know this hunger tormented her too.

It haunted her through her years in L.A., Paris,
and New York, the parties she went to, people
she met—Paul Robeson, Zora Neale Hurston,
Langston Hughes, Gertrude Stein. It haunts
her expression still, on the 6 train, Grand
Central station, an echo chamber behind
her eyes. But dear universe: if I can recognize
her face under this tunnel of endless shadows
against the luminance of all that is extinct
and oncoming, then I am not a stranger here.

Notes

"Oculus" in the first section is based on the story of a nineteen-year-old girl in Shanghai who uploaded her suicide onto Instagram in 2014.

"Provenance: A Vivisection" stems from the controversies surrounding the Bodies World Exhibitions, concerning the origins of the plastinated bodies on display and the implications that they belong to Chinese dissidents from corpse factories in China.

"The Toll of the Sea" rewrites the 1922 silent film starring Anna May Wong of the same name, directed by Chester Franklin. It is one of the first Technicolor films ever made, and the first successful Hollywood two-color Technicolor film—black and white with shades of red and green. The italicized lines quote directly from the film's lines.

"Anna May Wong Has Breakfast at Tiffany's" centers on the film *Breakfast at Tiffany's* (1961), directed by Blake Edwards, based on the Truman Capote novel. The film features a racist caricature, Mr. Yunioshi, played by Mickey Rooney in yellowface. Roland Winters, Sidney Toler, and Warner Oland were all white actors who made lifelong careers out of playing Asian characters in yellowface. The role they all had in common was Charlie Chan.

"Anna May Wong Blows Out Sixteen Candles" centers on the film *Sixteen Candles* (1984), directed by John Hughes. The biographical details are found in a biography of Anna May Wong, *Anna May Wong: From Laundryman's Daughter to Hollywood Legend* by Graham Russell Hodges (Hong Kong University Press, 2012).

"Electronic Motherland" refers to the Foxconn Riots in Taiyuan Province, China, in September 2012, when 2,000 workers rioted, shutting down the factory that manufactured electronics for computer companies like Apple and Dell. After a string of employee suicides in 2010, the company installed netting to catch the jumpers.

"The Mongolian Cow Sour Yogurt Super Voice Girl" is based on the hugely popular television show in China, broadcasted by Hunan Satellite Television between 2004 and 2006, of the same name. In the show, young women compete to become the next singer and idol of China. Winners were chosen based on an audience-voting process broadcasted across the country.

"Electronic Necropolis" is set in Guiyu Village, a village that specializes in mining and recycling electronic waste, such as computers and motherboards.

"The Diary of Afong Moy" is based on the history of Afong Moy, the first Chinese woman to travel to the United States in 1834. At nineteen, she was exhibited and displayed among various Chinese curiosities and objects, and spectators paid admission to see her. The exhibition was meant to sell Asian products to the American white middle class. She went on a tour through the United States, and visited Andrew Jackson's White House. In later years, Afong Moy is said to have been employed by P. T. Barnum. *The Barnum Years* section references a P. T. Barnum enterprise where Barnum brought over a family of six Chinese people from Canton to promote his new museum. In the description Barnum wrote of the new Chinese lady, he discredited Afong Moy: "the only other female ever known to have left the 'Central Flowery Nation' in order to visit the 'outside barbarians' [is] one of apocryphal reputation and position in her own country." This quote comes from *Ten Thousand Things on China and the Chinese* (1850). I also used the article by John Haddad, "The Chinese Lady and China for the Ladies: Race, Gender, and Public Exhibition in Jacksonian America," *Chinese America: History & Perspectives—The Journal of the Chinese Historical Society of America* (San Francisco: Chinese Historical Society of America with UCLA Asian American Studies Center, 2011: 5–19).

"Anna May Wong Meets Josephine Baker" imagines a meeting between Wong and Baker, who both moved to Europe in the 1920s to escape racial stereotyping in the United States.

"Anna May Wong Makes Cameos" references various films from the 2000s that contain Asian themes: *Romeo Must Die*, directed by Andrzej Bartkowiak; *Kill Bill*, directed by Quentin Tarantino; *The Last Samurai*, directed by Edward Zwick; "Hollaback Girl," a music video by Gwen Stefani; and *Memoirs of a Geisha*, directed by Rob Marshall.

"Anna May Wong Dreams of Wong Kar-Wai" refers to the plots of several films by Wong Kar-Wai, an iconic Hong Kong filmmaker, director of *In the Mood for Love*, *2046*, *Chungking Express*, *Happy Together*, *Fallen Angels*, and *Days of Being Wild*. Wong Kar-Wai's heroines are often heartbroken. "California Dreamin'" by The Mamas & the Papas is repeated throughout the film *Chungking Express*.

"Anna May Wong Stars as Cyborg #86" takes details from the film *Cloud Atlas* (2012), which employed Korean actresses as cyborgs in a future dystopic Asian city. Two white actors in *Cloud Atlas* wear yellowface with slanted eyes.

"Ghost in the Shell" refers to a 1989 manga by Masamune Shirow and 1995 futuristic Japanese anime directed by Mamoru Oshii whose story was adapted into a 2017 film by Paramount, which cast white actress Scarlett Johansson as Major, a Japanese character, to much public outcry.

"Dirge with Cutlery and Furs" is about the South Korean fashion model Daul Kim (1989–2009) who regularly kept a blog before she committed suicide in her Paris apartment in 2009. In her blog "I Like to Fork Myself," she chronicled life as a fashion model, beginning each post with "say hi to." In many posts, she was candid about her depression and loneliness. The last blog post was titled, "say hi to forever."

"Yume Miru Kikai [The Dreaming Machine]" is the title of the film that master animator Satoshi Kon never completed before his death, and the film that Madhouse Animation Studio has not yet finished due to budget issues. The borrowed lines are from Makiko Itoh's translation of Kon's last letter before he died of cancer in 2010, written on his blog, to his fans.

"The Five Faces of Faye Valentine" examines a character from *Cowboy Bebop*, an anime series directed by Shinichirō Watanabe. Faye Valentine is a fictional character, a poker player with a bounty on her head.

"Lavender Town" is a town in *Pokémon* where dead Pokémon are buried. There are multiple urban legends and myths surrounding this town, including a myth that tells of children driven to commit suicide after reaching this level on the Pokémon game.

"The Death of Ruan Lingyu" refers to the famous Chinese film actress Ruan Lingyu, whose suicide at the age of twenty-four rocked China and the world in 1935, following the release of her movie *New Women*, wherein she plays a writer who suffers a similar fate.

"After Nam June Paik" takes its subtitles from various pieces by Nam June Paik in the exhibition *Becoming Robot* at the Asia Society's 2014 exhibition in New York City. It also references a Paik piece on display at the Smithsonian National Art Museum, *Electronic Superhighway: Continental U.S., Alaska, Hawaii*. The section *Li Tai Po* takes its cento lines from poems by Li Po and lines from Janelle Monáe's songs "Oh, Maker" from her album *The ArchAndroid* (2011) and "Electric Lady" from her album *The Electric Lady* (2013). The section *Mall of the Electronic Superhighway* takes its James Baldwin quote from a Henry Louis Gates, Jr. interview with Baldwin and Josephine Baker in 1987, anthologized in the book *James Baldwin: The Legacy*, edited by Quincy Troupe (Simon and Schuster/Touchstone: New York, 1989: 172).

"Oculus" in the last section documents my experience at a performance, "An Ode To," by Solange Knowles at the Solomon R. Guggenheim Museum on May 18, 2017. The Guggenheim Museum is the world's most photographed place, according to the *Washington Post* and Google satellites, and the oculus on the top of the museum is an iconic window envisioned by Frank Lloyd Wright. In a 1955 letter to the then-director of the museum, Wright asks, "Isn't a picture (like sculpture and like a building) a circumstance in nature; sharing light and dark—warm and cold—changing with every subtle change: seen now in one light; now in another?"

"Resurrection" refers to a 2014 exhibition *Chinese American: Exclusion/Inclusion* at the New-York Historical Society focusing on the history of Chinese immigration in America, which prominently displayed Anna May Wong's face on its posters and advertisements around New York City.

Acknowledgments

I am grateful to the following publications and their editors, where versions of these poems have found homes:

Bat City Review: "The Mongolian Cow Sour Yogurt Super Voice Girl"

Black Warrior Review: "Yume Miru Kikai [The Dreaming Machine]"

BOMB: "Anna May Wong Goes Viral," "The Death of Ruan Lingyu"

Crazyhorse: "Occidentalism"

Four Way Review: "Oculus," "Mutant Odalisque"

Harvard Review Online: "Provenance: A Vivisection"

Hyphen: "Anna May Wong on Silent Films," "Anna May Wong Has Breakfast at Tiffany's"

jubilat: "After Nam June Paik": *Opera Sextronique, Li Tai Po,* and *Mall of the Electronic Superhighway*

Kenyon Review Online: "Close Encounters of the Liminal Kind"

Linebreak: "Dirge with Cutlery and Furs"

The Margins: "Anna May Wong Goes Home with Bruce Lee," "Lavender Town," "After Nam June Paik": *Good Morning Mr. Orwell*

The Missouri Review: "Anna May Wong Fans Her Time Machine," "Anna May Wong Meets Josephine Baker," "Anna May Wong Blows Out Sixteen Candles," "Anna May Wong Makes Cameos," "Anna May Wong Rates the Runway"

Poetry: "The Toll of the Sea"

Poets.org *Poem-a-Day:* "Riding Alone for Thousands of Miles," "Resurrection"

A Public Space: "Ghost Story"

Puerto del Sol: "Antipode Essay"

Salt Hill:	"Anna May Wong Stars as Cyborg #86"
Third Coast:	"Electronic Necropolis"
Tin House:	"Teledildonics"
Washington Square Review:	"Live Feed," "Anna May Wong Dreams of Wong Kar-Wai"

"Anna May Wong Blows Out Sixteen Candles" was selected for a Pushcart Prize in the 2017 *Pushcart Prize XLI: Best of the Small Presses* anthology.

I would like to sincerely thank the following organizations, residencies, fellowships, and institutions for their generous resources, valuable time, and community, without which the writing of this book would not be possible: the Dorothy and Lewis B. Cullman Center for Scholars and Writers at the New York Public Library, the Jenny McKean Moore Writer-in-Washington program at the George Washington University, the Singapore Creative Writing Residency, the National University of Singapore, the Singapore Arts House, the Saltonstall Foundation, Hedgebrook, Vermont Studio Center, the Jerome Foundation, Bread Loaf Writers' Conference, and the Cornell University English Department.

I harbor the deepest gratitude to my teachers, mentors, and community, whose steadfast support moves me to believe in what's possible. Thank you to my teachers and mentors: Terrance Hayes, Alice Fulton, Lyrae Van-Clief Stefanon, Dave Eggers, Vendela Vida, Kenneth McClane, and Yona Harvey. This manuscript began while I was at Cornell. Thank you to the incredible friends and fellow writers who have supported me and conversed with me as I worked on this manuscript—thank you for being true when I am down, up, and everything in between. Ocean Vuong for the late-night conversations, endless cups of tea, and frolicking in the snow, Cathy Linh Che for your eyes on this manuscript and for the international adventures, Jane Wong for the conversations about our ghosts and discovering wild girl poetics together, Jennifer Chang for being my mentor-sister and champion. Thank you to Jen Lue, Emily Jungmin Yoon, Madeleine Barnes, Soham Patel, Thora Siemson, Jenny Xie, Dan Lau, and so many others in my community for the vast amounts of love and support. Thank you Lisa Page for the wonderful welcome to GWU and tarot card readings. Thank you to my colleagues and friends at the Cullman Center, especially

Jean Strouse, Lauren Goldenberg, Angela Flournoy, Nicole Fleetwood, and Saidiya Hartman: you are my role models, and it was a privilege to be at the Cullman Center with you. To my community at Kundiman: *if it were not so.* Thank you to Joseph Legaspi and Sarah Gambito for first bringing me into this poetry family. Thank you to my family—my father, Ming Mao, and my mother, Hong Li, my grandmother, aunts and uncles, who have crossed so many borders to get here.

I am also indebted to the long line of writers and artists, living and departed, who have come before me. I find this book in conversation with many of my heroes and artistic influences—Ai, June Jordan, Federico Garcia Lorca, Bei Dao, Shu Ting, Qiu Miaojing, Nam June Paik, Lucille Clifton, Audre Lorde, Satoshi Kon, Yayoi Kusama, Ana Mendieta, Frida Kahlo, Wong Kar-Wai, Maxine Hong Kingston, Marilyn Chin, Theresa Hak Kyung Cha, Edwidge Danticat, Jamaica Kincaid, Claudia Rankine, James Baldwin, Toni Morrison, and many others. Also cheers to my icons and muses who have appeared in this book: Anna May Wong, Josephine Baker, Rihanna, Janelle Monáe, and Solange.

Thank you to Jeff Shotts for your brilliance, vision, and patience, and to Fiona McCrae and the whole staff and team at Graywolf Press who have given this book the ultimate chance to live. Thank you to Karen Gu, who always sends me books and the best cards and notes and has been a champion of the project in a way I never imagined possible.

I wrote this book for women of color. Without you, the world isn't possible. Because of you, I keep going. I have learned this the hard way: you matter, and don't let anyone or anything convince you otherwise.

SALLY WEN MAO was born in Wuhan, China, and raised in northern California. She is the author of a previous collection of poems, *Mad Honey Symposium*, a *Poets & Writers* Top Ten Debut Poetry Collection of 2014. She was a Dorothy and Lewis B. Cullman Center Fellow at the New York Public Library and a Jenny McKean Moore Writer-in-Washington at the George Washington University. Her work has won a Pushcart Prize, a Jerome Foundation grant, an Amy Award from *Poets & Writers*, and has appeared in *Poetry*, *A Public Space*, *Tin House*, *The Best of the Net 2014*, and *The Best American Poetry 2013*, among others. She holds an M.F.A. from Cornell University and has taught writing and poetry at Cornell University, Hunter College, the National University of Singapore, the George Washington University, and other spaces. The first poem she wrote in second grade was about summer.

www.sallywenmao.com
@sallywenmao

This book is made possible through a partnership with the College of Saint Benedict, and honors the legacy of S. Mariella Gable, a distinguished teacher at the College.

Previous titles in this series include:

Loverboy by Victoria Redel

The House on Eccles Road by Judith Kitchen

One Vacant Chair by Joe Coomer

The Weatherman by Clint McCown

Collected Poems by Jane Kenyon

Variations on the Theme of an African Dictatorship by Nuruddin Farah:
    Sweet and Sour Milk
    Sardines
    Close Sesame

Duende by Tracy K. Smith

All of It Singing: New and Selected Poems by Linda Gregg

The Art of Syntax: Rhythm of Thought, Rhythm of Song by Ellen Bryant Voigt

How to Escape from a Leper Colony by Tiphanie Yanique

One Day I Will Write About This Place by Binyavanga Wainaina

The Convert: A Tale of Exile and Extremism by Deborah Baker

On Sal Mal Lane by Ru Freeman

Citizen: An American Lyric by Claudia Rankine

On Immunity: An Inoculation by Eula Biss

Cinder: New and Selected Poems by Susan Stewart

The Art of Death: Writing the Final Story by Edwidge Danticat

A Lucky Man by Jamel Brinkley

Support for this series has been provided by the Manitou Fund as part of the Warner Reading Program.

The text of *Oculus* is set in Adobe Garamond Pro.
Book design by Rachel Holscher.
Composition by Bookmobile Design and Digital
Publisher Services, Minneapolis, Minnesota.
Manufactured by Versa Press on acid-free,
30 percent postconsumer wastepaper.